Somewhere in the Sky

Self-Exploration

Karolee Krause, LPC, SAC

Preface

Through a compilation of everyday travel, food foraging, and stories about human nature, learn to incorporate gratitude, laughter, hope and inspiration into your own life.

As a Licensed Professional Counselor, author and traveler, Karolee shares inspirational stories and guidance to inspire, motivate and encourage you to follow and embark upon your own everyday adventures to a healthier and happier life.

The Journey Begins

I frequently help people move out of their comfort zones and take calculated risks in life.

For years, I focused on my career and took little time off to travel or explore. My life had become stagnant and I had to get out of my comfort zone. To do so, I booked a solo and group trip to Havasu Falls where I overcame fear, various anxieties, and faced new challenges and life experiences.

What holds you back from living your dream?

Are you long overdue for an adventure?

Havasu Falls

Traveling Solo

Have you ever tried traveling solo? Venturing forth alone feeds your soul like no other experience. By traveling alone, you learn new skills, find your unexpected strengths, and connect with others who share your passions. Find your own path today, one where you travel alone in the presence of others.

Where would you travel solo if you could go anywhere?

What are your hopes and fears about traveling solo?

Tigertail Beach

Blossom and Grow

Where are you growing? Are there parts of you that seek growth through new experiences or opportunities? Growth happens on many levels including the emotional, mental, physical and spiritual.

Learn to blossom like a flower, easily, beautifully and naturally.

Where do you need growth the most?

Where are you resisting it?

Flourish

Before I Die

In Asheville, North Carolina there was a **Before I Die** wall. The artist's concept was to create a space for people to write down what they wanted to do before they died. There were a variety of answers written on the wall including: spend more time with mother, see the end of terrorism, fly an airplane, fear nothing, end hate, be happy, love with all my heart, eat 500 hotdogs and get baptized.

What do you want to do before you die?

How motivated are you to do it while you are still able?

Asheville

What Makes You Unique?

Most of us like to blend into the crowd, yet we all have our unique strengths and traits that set us apart from each other. Sometimes we forget what our personal traits are and need to be reminded.

Whatever sets you apart from others, identify it, celebrate it, and share it with others and own it!

What makes you unique and stand out from the crowd?

How can you use your unique gifts and talents in a way that helps others?

Stormy Weather

Life can, and often becomes stormy and difficult. How you weather the storm is up to you. Sometimes the storms seem never ending but eventually even the heaviest of storm clouds disappear, giving way to a new day. Remember when you are in the eye of the storm, that it too shall pass and the remaining storms temporary. Recognize that storms, like the rain, gives new life to the old or outdated parts of our lives.

If you are experiencing storminess in your life, look at what needs to be released or let go. Trust that the storm will pass and that the sun will shine again.

What's the hardest thing you have ever lived through?

How did it empower you?

Where Are You Growing?

Sometimes we find ourselves in difficult circumstances or situations, including unfulfilling and unhappy relationships or dead-end jobs. Sometimes our life situations feel unbearable, but often when we find ourselves in the hardest of places, we have the opportunity to learn to grow the most.

Next time you find your life's circumstances restricting, remember that your soul planted you in this place for a reason, and that you have been offered an opportunity to heal or grow.

In what areas of your life do you need to grow?

How will you facilitate that growth?

Soul Searching

How much of your life have you spent searching for something or someone but have come up empty? Are you seeking a life partner, climbing the ladder of success, or searching for a place to belong? It's so easy to get lost in the search that we often forget where we are, or even worse, who we are.

Instead of searching or seeking outside of yourself for someone or something, travel within, and seek an inner connection with yourself. Stop grasping and searching, and you will ultimately find what you truly need in life.

What do you seek in life?

Of what you seek, what aspects already exist within you?

Somewhere in the Sky

Raw Wild Blackberries

As a Counselor, I often talk with my clients about the body/mind connection and explain that when we feed our body poorly, we also don't feel well emotionally or mentally. Food is nature's medicine, and it is often neglected by most of us. As of late, there seems to be a reawakened interest in going natural and focusing on health and nutrition again.

I am always seeking everyday adventures, and often go in search of them on my bicycle. On one of my bike rides, I found miles of wild blackberries. I parked my bike alongside some of them and started munching on berries straight from the bushes themselves.

What areas in your life do you need to go natural?

How can you be more adventurous in your daily travels?

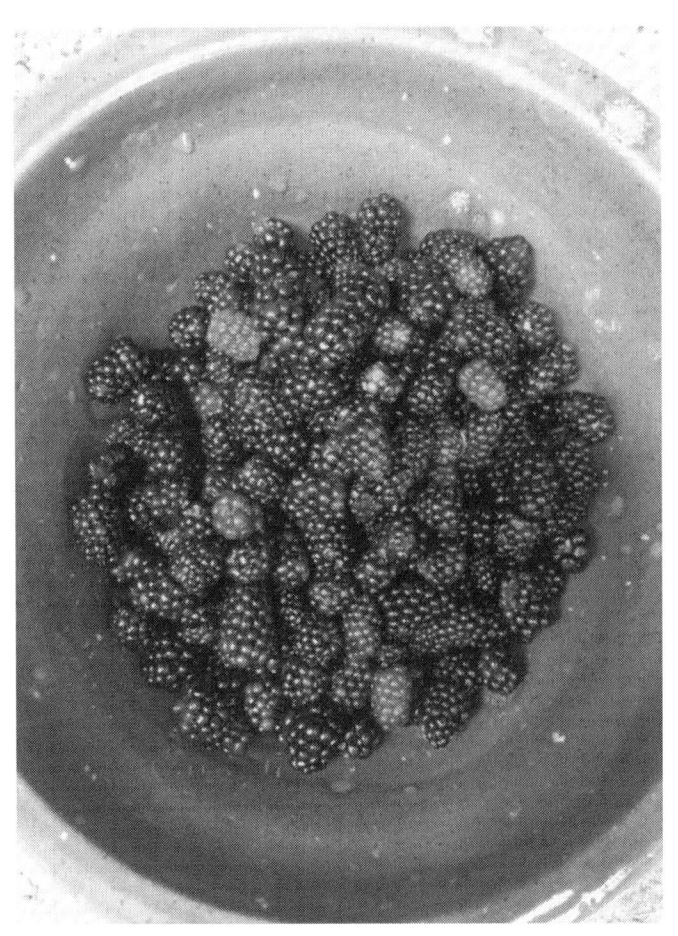

Planting Smiles

Research tells us that smiling improves our health and creates happy hormones in our brains. Smiling even transforms anger and negativity. Smiling when you least feel like it can lift your mood and steer you back to a happier state of mind.

Today, set an intention to smile at as many people as you can, or simply smile at one person. Sometimes it's the people who don't smile that are the ones who need it the most.

Has anyone ever smiled at you when you most needed it?

Do you randomly smile at others? If not, start today. You could make a difference in someone's life.

Make Someone Smile

The Psychology of Fun

Play has physical and mental health benefits. Research indicates that play helps relieve stress and depression symptoms by releasing endorphins that make you feel good. Play also increases your energy levels and immune system.

There are many ways to play. It doesn't matter which activity you participate in, but what's important is that you make the time to play as a part of your daily schedule. There are a million ways to play!

What is your favorite way to play?

Schedule time in your day to play, even if it's for only 10 minutes.

Rosholt Fun Fair

Marco Island

Hidden among modern condominiums and high-rise hotels on Marco Island, Florida, lies a hidden treasure called Tigertail Beach. Secluded from urban America and detached from the stresses of life, this beautiful beach is a magical place where earth meets sea.

When you arrive, you can either walk along the pristine white sandy beach, or you can cross the lagoon, wading waist deep through warm salty waters. You will find yourself among southern Florida's unique wildlife including tropical fish, ospreys, egrets, and dolphins.

After you cross the lagoon, walk a sandy trail that leads you out to the oceanfront, where you can walk and explore three miles of beautiful wild, unspoiled natural beach discover yourself through nature.

What is the wildest adventure that you have ever had?

How adventurous are you in nature? Do you find seclusion healing?

Marco Island

The Healing Labyrinth

At times in our daily lives, we become lost or directionless and may find ourselves seeking guidance. I created the Healing Labyrinth for people in our community to have a place to walk, reflect, meditate and to spend time within. In the center of the labyrinth, the tree of life grows, adorned with beautiful prayer ribbons.

As you walk mindfully in the labyrinth, seek guidance. Be open to direction when you arrive in the center; when you walk out, take what you have learned into the world with you.

How do you personally go within?

Where and when do you seek guidance?

Stevens Point Sculpture Park

End of Trail

The journey to the "End of Trail", was an adventure of courage, guidance, and self-exploration. After climbing for several hours in the hills and mountains around Sedona, Arizona, I eventually reached the the summit. I could not go any further.

I looked out over the beautiful Arizona landscape, feeling the grounding rock beneath my feet. As I sat on top of the rock, I reflected on own my path, literally and symbolically. Had I reached the "End of Trail" in other areas of my life as well?

At different times in our lives, we arrive at the end of the trail and have to start a new path or journey. Life continually takes us to the "End of Trail". It is during these times that we need to look back, reflect, be thankful, and search for the next trail in our life.

If we learn where to look, there are always new paths to explore, mountains to climb, and people to help guide us along the way.

Have you ever hit a dead end? What did you do?

Sedona, Arizona

Exploring the Unknown

Years ago, I joined eight strangers on a hiking trip to Utah, where we spent four days exploring exotic landscapes, climbing the cliffs of the world's largest sandstone canyons and connecting with one another. The hike was much more difficult than I had expected, but well worth the climb to see beautiful new places.

Is something calling out to you to be explored?

Do you need to go alone or with others?

How does the challenge feed your heart and soul?

What is the payoff for you when you explore?

Self-Exploration

Nature and Nurture

When you're feeling out of balance, take yourself out into nature. Research confirms that nature is a natural healer. The fresh air, sunshine, and the earth beneath our feet are all healing.

If you can't get outside, bring life indoors. Surround yourself with potted plants, flowers, or create a small rock garden.

How can you make your home more healing?

What simple thing can you do to create positive change in your life?

Laughter Therapy

The benefits of laughter, even during the darkest of times, brings light to our suffering. Laughing doesn't take away from the seriousness of our hardships, but it can help us get through stressful times by providing much-needed relief.

Start each day by setting an intention to laugh, even for a few minutes. Laugh with your friends, your family members, or pet. Laughing feels great, even if at first you may not feel like it. Laugh your way to a better and healthier you!

Do you need more laughter in your life?

Would the people around you benefit from seeing you laugh?

How will you incorporate more laughter into your daily life?

Laughter is Contagious

Therapeutic Landscapes

Did you know that different geographical locations or landscapes can be spiritually or physically healing? The next time you travel, tune into the elements.

Every geographical location has its own energy, its own ecosystem, and its own natural vibration. **Mountains** represent strength and stability. **Deserts** are ancient and sacred places to journey within yourself. **Forests** are magical places where green plants and trees heal. **Oceans** and saltwater replenish our spirit, while salt air cleanses our lungs.

The next time you plan a trip, think about geographical locations, and let your body, mind, and spirit guide you.

Is there a special place calling you?

At home, take Epsom salt baths and use mud facial scrubs for cleansing and healing.

Golden Canyon

Sacred Traveler's Bucket List

There are travelers, and then there are sacred travelers, those who have a deep connection to the earth and a desire to experience it all: the deserts, mountains, oceans, and forests of the world. We hear the call of faraway distant lands and have a love of their landscapes and people. Sacred travelers also find passion in other people's journeys.

Are you a sacred traveler, and if so, what or where is calling you?

How do you take the steps to becoming a sacred traveler?

Costa Rica

Life in Kefalonia

One of my first overseas trips was to Athens, Greece when I also backpacked through Italy, Austria, France, and England.

Athens was hot and crowded and my backpack felt like it grew heavier with each step I took while hiking there. While traveled around Europe that summer, I ended up throwing shirts, shorts, and dresses into city garbage bins across several countries. I had packed too much stuff into my small bag.

Make today the day that you clear out your home, office or head. Travel lightly, wherever you are.

What do you carry in your day-to-day life that needs to be released or thrown away?

Kefalonia, Greece

Adventures in Community Service

In tropical Costa Rica, I had the opportunity to participate in community service, which involved painting a local resident's house in exchange for a homemade Costa Rican meal. I had never painted a house before, nor had I painted a house in the rain or around a termite's nest, but it turned out to be an adventure into giving back and learning about a new culture.

There are millions of ways to give back and it feels great!

What can you do to help someone in your neighborhood, or community?

Do you have creative talents that you can teach others?

Mexican Sleeping Pods

Landing in Mexico City, Mexico, I was excited to spend the night in a sleeping pod, located in Terminal 1 at Aeropuerto Internacional Benito Juárez airport. The pod included WiFi, TV, and air conditioning. Showers and lockers are also included along with complimentary socks and earplugs. The pod was comfortable and clean, and the mattress and pillow were made out of memory foam. The pod was private, cozy, and comfortable.

What has been the craziest or most enjoyable new experience in travel that you have ever had?

What new adventures lie in your future?

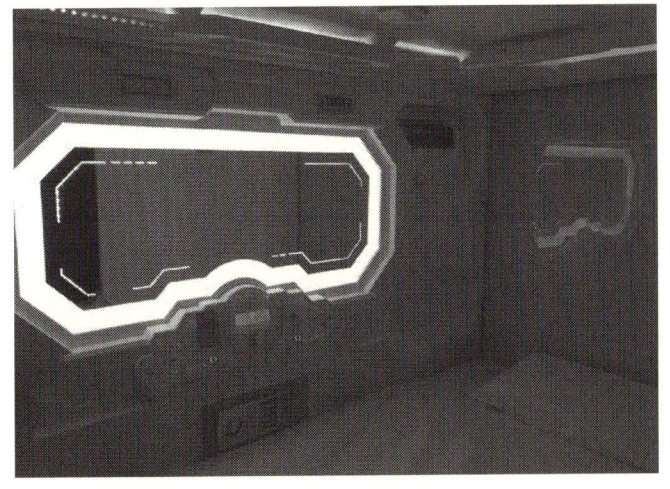

Mexico City

Salt Flats

Death Valley is a world where the average daytime temperature rises above 100 degrees Fahrenheit and where life can vanish in the baking sun. Not for those who are faint of heart, this harsh desert is a beautiful place that is as diverse as it is dangerous. Among other experiences in Death Valley, I found myself below sea level on the badland salt flats, hiking to a hidden waterfall and watching the sunset over the painted mural mountains.

Sometimes in life what we expect isn't always what we get.

Where have you gone and discovered that it was much better than you expected?

Badwater Basin

Tolantongo Mexico

One of my favorite places on earth lays hidden away in northern Mexico. Full of waterfall caves and thermal hot springs, Tolantongo is a place that warms the soul and body. Entailing one flight, three rural bus trips and no hotel reservation, I arrived and discovered a geographic spa that washed away every bit of stress I had ever carried as I soaked in the healing thermal waters of Tolantongo.

Nature is a powerful healer.

If you haven't found one yet, maybe it's time to make some plans to go. Where will you travel to next to heal yourself?

What has been the most healing place that you have ever been to?

Random People

Hiking in Death Valley in heat over 100 degrees and having survived, we arrived at the visitor's center. I wanted to take a photo of the outside thermometer. Because Death Valley is one of the hottest places in the United States, several other people were taking pictures as well, so I decided to snap this photo (opposite page) of random people.

When traveling, we often capture people and strangers in our photographs. Looking at their photographs, I think about their lives. Are they happy? Are they having fun? Do they like each other? Did someone force them to go on the trip? Am I in their photos? Do they wonder about me or my life?

Have you ever connected with random strangers on a trip and become friends?

How did you connect and how did your life paths cross?

A Minimalist Journey

Taking steps to live a minimalist life may not be easy but it is liberating as you become free from the past and your life becomes lighter in ways that you could never imagine.

After relocating several times across the country, I made the decision that I did not want a lot of material baggage in my life anymore. I had spent too much of my time and energy accumulating things. Most everything had to go, so I donated most of my belongings to charity and lightened my load.

Take one step today to clear old clutter from your home, basement, or office. You will be amazed at how the new space opens up possibilities!

What can you release today that will make your life easier and simpler?

What can you throw out or leave behind?

Naples

The *New York Times* Cat House

As I finished writing an article for publication, I placed the newspaper on the floor next to my bags, for recycling. My cat quickly jumped in and made a house out of it. He enjoyed his house so much that he played in the paper for several days.

Next time you move to automatically throw something away or as it heads to the recycling bin, ask yourself, what else can this be used for? There are probably a thousand and one other uses for it!

How can you be more efficient at recycling to help your community and the earth as a whole?

How can you be more creative with your recyclables?

Mental Decluttering

I began the process of decluttering my life years ago as I released my collection of worthless possessions and sent them off to Goodwill.

During the process of simplifying my life and working toward a goal of minimalism, I realized material clutter was only a part of the problem.

The real issue was going to be decluttering my mind and thinking process.

As a thinker, I realized that I could empty my house, but my head was still full of clutter. So, I began meditating to unclutter my mind.

Simplifying life begins with the process of both internal and external purging. Learn the practice of clearing your mind by simply sitting in silence every day for 5 minutes, then extend the time by a minute each week. Eventually you will find the silence a welcome break as you declutter your mind and find inner peace.

What can you do to start decluttering your mind and your thought processes?

Find Inner Peace

Chicken Therapy

I was unfamiliar with Chicken Therapy until I met a woman who had eleven pet chickens. The chickens were a variety of colors and breeds and all had their own names.

Chickens, the owner told me, have distinct personalities just like people. Some chickens are curious, playful or even adventurous, while others are shy and timid. All chickens, though, are unique.

After a stressful weekend, I asked her if I could hold one of her chickens, and was handed a beautiful, soft golden-brown bird. As I held the feathery clucking chicken in my arms, I felt an immediate sense of peace and calm.

Chicken Therapy is not commonly known, but it exists, and research confirms that chickens make great therapy animals. Next time you're having a bad day and feeling sad, anxious, or frustrated, try some Chicken Therapy!

What animals in your life make you feel better about your day?

Thank You!

I was envious of people living in the tropics who have mango, coconut, orange, lemon, or lime trees in their yards. On the other hand, I lived in a condo and often saw mangoes and other fruit rotting on the ground in my neighborhood. I wondered why people did not give their fruit away for free. Isn't it better to share your abundance than to allow it to go to waste?

One day driving down a new street, I saw a box of mangoes on the side of the road with a sign that said, "free". I quickly pulled over and excitedly picked four large mangoes out of the box.

I was grateful to the person who was offering to share their abundance with strangers. That same morning, I drove back to the box of mangoes and left a thank you note to let them know how grateful I was for their generosity.

What do you have that you can share with others?

Gratitude

Diversity of Life

"Life is like a tomato. When it falls to the ground, it begins to rot," Dooley explained. "Life rots unless we experience different things and have new adventures."

I was inspired by Dooley's perspective on life, a man who celebrates diversity. Dooley teaches inmates in prison, helping them achieve their GED diplomas. He expressed that his inspiration was to help redirect prisoners' lives. He said he always goes to work being "hopeful" and said that he retains hope in even the most difficult situations.

Dooley had a great attitude toward life and says that his message is to "Stay positive and move forward."

How do you spread hope to others?

When has someone else made you feel hopeful about a situation or outcome?

Dooley

Navajo Country

I knew that I was traveling to a remote part of the country, but I didn't realize how far I was traveling until I boarded a flight out of Phoenix on a tiny Pilatus PC-12 aircraft that seated eight passengers maximum, and which would eventually land on top of the White Mountains in Arizona.

Before I had even left on my latest adventure, I was informed that I would be tired as I adjusted to an elevation of over 7,000 feet. my body would have to build red blood cells to more efficiently deliver oxygen to my body as it adjusted to the thin atmosphere.

Mountain life was different from what I was accustomed to, and offered a raw natural beauty, aromatic ponderosa pines, pristine lakes and rivers. One of my favorite memories was driving down the mountain road as wild horses in a nearby field ran next to my car.

What is the most remote place that you have ever visited?

Do you dream of living remote and if so, what calls you there?

White Mountains

Seeking Solitude

As a traveler, I always seek solitude in beautiful, natural locations where I can leave life far behind. Quite unexpectedly on a recent trip to Cape Cod, I found seclusion on a beautiful and remote beach where the rest of the world ceased to exist.

After trekking for several miles on sandy coastal dunes, I found a deserted spot perched high up on an ocean cliff where the only sound was that of crashing waves on a rocky seashore, and where seals played in the ocean's surf.

The Atlantic wind carried my mind a million miles away as I imagined what it would be like to spend a year on this secluded shore away from a world overrun with people.

Do you seek isolation in nature?

Where is your favorite spot to just think and be?

Cape Cod

The World of Herbs

Native Americans use native plants to treat ailments of all kinds and for a variety of other health concerns. Research indicates that approximately sixty percent of the medicines we use today come from native herbs.

For example, caffeine free herbal teas are now commonly consumed for a variety of symptoms including insomnia, digestive issues, hormonal issues, and to enhance memory and mood. Such a simple yet healing remedy can now be found in your local grocery store. Making your own teas is also easy.

Do you use natural herbs or plants in your diet?

How can you incorporate more of these healing foods into your everyday life?

Mountain Teas

Funky Flagstaff

I discovered Flagstaff, a funky and fun mountain town one day as I was traveling on a hiking trip to the Grand Canyon.

Flagstaff sits at an elevation of 6,909 feet in the San Francisco Peaks of the Rocky Mountains. This alternative town is full of tasty ethnic restaurants, vibrational sound healing, and a fabulous tea house that offers Japanese style seating and lavender mint lattes in a new age setting like no other.

Have you ever found or explored a place that took you by surprise?

Where was it and what about it inspired you?

How can you make your own home or environment more colorful or interesting?

Flagstaff

Sin City Mindfulness

Las Vegas is probably the last place where you would expect to experience mindfulness, but it turned out to be the perfect place for me to spend three bliss-filled days of silence and peace when I attended a workshop on advanced mindfulness.

On the rooftop of a Las Vegas Hotel, I practiced mindful walking, felt the autumn breeze, watched a tiny feather floating in the swimming pool, and observed jet airplanes soaring in the sky. The world as I knew it had come to a standstill and the stillness that I entered within, was a place of peace that drowned out other city noises. Gone was the world outside filled with chaos, honking horns, and swarms of people.

You don't have to go anywhere to find peace or silence. You only have to travel within.

Have you ever heard the silence of your own soul?

Start a simple mindfulness practice. The peace you seek is always there, wherever you are.

Las Vegas

Oxygen O2 Bar

In the middle of Phoenix, I unexpectedly found myself standing in front of an oxygen bar. Having driven to the city, a trip of almost 200 miles down the mountains and with an elevation drop of over 5,000 feet in altitude, and still struggling to acclimate to the region, I thought the oxygen bar would provide me with an added boost of energy.

Once inside, I learned that oxygen aids oneself by boosting energy levels, reducing stress and toxins in the body, and increasing concentration and focus. Natural oils, such as lavender and eucalyptus, could be added to the oxygen to enhance the experience and to create a feeling of relaxation or as an energy boost. I laid down on a massage bed and relaxed as I breathed in the aromatherapy oil into my lungs and felt a new sense of life enter my tired and depleted body. I enjoyed the new experience and felt the benefits of a much-needed boost.

What kind of new experiences have you had lately?

If you haven't had any new experiences, make it a goal to do something new.

Phoenix

Life in Transition

What do you do when life challenges you in unexpected ways? Drive a U-Haul across country and leave behind the life you know and start anew.

Driving a 20-foot U-Haul and towing a car was completely out of my comfort zone. My travel companion reminded me to breathe as I began the journey by driving the truck the wrong way into rural mountains with no place to turn around. I white-knuckled the steering wheel as I drove further into the unfamiliar mountain range.

For four days, we were enchanted by New Mexico's beauty, laughed across Texas and wanted to kill each other in the cattle fields of Kansas. We survived, recognizing our adventure was a test of strength, endurance, and patience. We ate Chinese in Super 8 Hotels and saw Dorothy's Wizard of Oz house near a trailer court in Kansas.

Have you ever had to start your life over?

If you had to, what would you do?

What would you do differently from your current life?

New Mexico

The Spiritual Path

After a life transition, I felt the call to quiet contemplation and spiritual direction and found myself driving to St. Anthony's Spiritual Sanctuary, a Franciscan retreat in rural Wisconsin.

I had no real plans, other than to spend a day in silent prayer and mindful walking; however, after I arrived, I met with the Reverend and spent time talking about life transitions and spiritual practice. I roamed the sanctuary, mesmerized by the long hallways that hundreds of young men who had walked there before me as they prepared for a lifetime devoted to spiritual practice.

Sometimes we feel as though we have to journey far to find a retreat or place of solitude, but the reality is that sanctuary is often closer than we think. The silence, the serenity, and tranquility that we seek is within each of us.

In life, sometimes we choose a path, and sometimes the path is chosen for us.

What is your chosen spiritual practice?

Are you in search of one?

The Art of Detachment

Watching Tibetan Monks creating a beautiful mandala out of colored sand was a meditational experience in itself. The mandala is a symbol of the universe, created in a circular shape to represent universal connection. After creating the mandala for several days or weeks, the monks mindfully and meticulously wipe the sand away, representing detachment and transience as the lesson.

Unless practiced, detachment is difficult thing to do. Think of something in your life that you can say goodbye to, let go of, or detach from. What are you holding onto that is causing you pain, creating suffering or preventing you from truly being happy?

Impermanence is a fact of life. Today embrace what brings you joy and happiness, as no one is guaranteed tomorrow. Through the art of detachment, we free ourselves from unhealthy suffering and live in the moment, a beautiful lesson from Tibetan teachings.

What is one thing that you can say or do for someone who you take for granted?

Paine Art Center

Drink of the Gods

Cocoa has commonly been known as the "Drink of the Gods" and has been around for more than one thousand years. Most people have a passion for chocolate or cocoa but have not had the experience of seeing this exotic bean in its raw, natural form.

On a previous trip to a Costa Rican Organic Eco-Farm, I had the opportunity to walk the grounds of the plantation, which consisted of over 300 cocoa trees.

The process of roasting and grinding fermented cocoa beans begins by using an ancient stone, called a "metate". The stones are carved by indigenous people out of volcanic rock. Once grinding the cocoa beans is completed, a variety of new world ingredients such as vanilla, allspice, spicy chile, achiote or annatto is added to make a flavorful spicy drink!

What have you had for food adventures in finding, making or tasting?

Humane Cuisine

Does it matter to you where your food comes from? Do you prefer local produce over food that has to be shipped from a distance? Does the quality of life of the animal you eat matter?

Farmers markets are a popular place for buying and selling organic produce that is locally grown. Grocery stores offer the choice of grass-fed beef and cage free eggs. People no longer want animals that are full of antibiotics or hormones and more people are become aware of the effects of unsustainable and cruel practices, like veal farming.

As a health-conscious person who cares about what you eat, know where your food comes from or if it is humanely raised. What we eat directly affects our own health. Animals kept in confinement or traumatized cause negative energy. The foods we eat affect us in more ways than one. Choose humanely raised animals. Choose to care.

How do you support humane farming practices or businesses that protect animals?

Choose to Be Humane

Architecture Meets Nature

In Spring Green, Wisconsin, the home of Frank Lloyd Wright's *Taliesin*, I explored The House on the Rock, an amazing design created by Alex Jordan Jr. According to history, Jordan shared his architectural vision with Wright who scoffed at him saying he wouldn't trust him to build a "cheese crate or chicken coop". The exchange led Jordan to build the house on the rock out of resentment.

Although the house now has numerous additional attractions and collections, I found the original Japanese style house built into the rocks mesmerizing. Giant metal cooking pots hang in the rock-enclosed kitchen and red velvet couches are nestled discretely within dark wooden libraries built directly into the sandstone, making it a haven for those seeking to combine architecture and nature.

Has anyone ever challenged you in a way that inspired you to prove them wrong?

How did this exchange empower you?

How might you create something great out of something negative in your life?

House on the Rock

Desert Cities

I landed at Phoenix Sky Harbor Airport at 10:00 p.m. The temperature was still a stifling 98 degrees Fahrenheit. At 8:30 a.m. the next morning, temperatures were already in the 90s, but wanting to explore Phoenix, and being a nature lover, I headed for the Desert Botanical Gardens where I began exploring the Sonoran Desert.

The gardens were beautiful as I walked the paths and trails to different parts of the park, checking out the variety of plants that grow in the hottest and driest parts of the world. I saw blooming cactus and nesting Inca doves, and spent time reflecting in the Contemplation Garden. Although beautiful, the Sonoran Desert was also a rough reminder of how dangerous the desert can be.

Have you ever traveled to a completely different geographical location?

If so, how did it challenge you in different ways?

Desert Botanical Garden

Mindful Meals

Being mindful of healthy foods is the first step but being aware of who you are eating your meals with and where you eat, is just as important as the food you put into your body.

It's during mealtime that we can practice mindful eating.

The next time you sit down to eat, look at your food closely. Consider the colors and textures, the smell, the aroma, and take mindful bites. Chew your food slowly and consciously, and finally enjoy the company you are eating with. Surround yourself with happy people, as they aid in good digestion. Eating not only nourishes our bodies, but it nourishes the soul.

When was the last time you tasted, smelled, or enjoyed your food?

Rainforest Cafe

Mexican Street Corn

When traveling through Mexico, I found myself drooling over the sight and smell of Mexican sweet corn being prepared and sold on city streets. There is something appetizing and exciting about eating authentic food with home grown ingredients.

What's your favorite street food?

How can you create your favorite food truck or street food at home with your family or friends?

Adventure Cuisine

On an adventure kayaking trip to the Apostle Islands, I had the opportunity to eat lunch in a wet suit on the sandy shores of Lake Superior.

It was the first time I ate lunch in the water. The food was tasty, but what was more appetizing was the environment itself. I have also eaten on mountain tops, in the rainforest, deserts and in the snow.

Adventures in food or food foraging are not only tasty, but fun!

Where is the most unusual place you have ever eaten?

If you can't travel to exotic places, plan a picnic in your backyard, or nearby park.

Apostle Islands

Witches Gulch

Only accessible by boat, Witches Gulch, a narrow slot canyon in southern Wisconsin is an interesting and beautiful hike that makes you wonder if you are still in the Midwest. At some points along the way you can actually touch both sides of the narrow canyon as you make your way down the darkened trail.

I'm not a big fan of narrow spaces even though I have hiked through slot canyons in some of the national parks out west. Unlike the dry desert terrain of the southwest, Wisconsin Dells is green, lush, and humid. The slot canyons are cool and temperate due to the running river and waterfall, making for an easy hike.

What is the toughest hike or trail that you have ever traveled on or through?

Are you an adventure seeker?

Where would you go and what kind of adventure would you have?

Sunbaked Fruit

On one of my everyday hiking trips through the forest, I came across a patch of wild blackberries. They provided me with a tasty afternoon snack as I munched on the berries straight off the bush.

What ever happened to eating raw and wild? Natural foods are free of pesticides and plastic packaging materials. When living in southern Florida, I picked and ate a small pineapple that was growing alongside some palm trees. The pineapple was warm, full of flavor, and tasted like sunshine.

Being in nature is healing in itself but finding natural foods and eating them off the tree, branch or ground is a true tasty adventure.

Have you ever gone in search of wild berries, or any other fruit or veggie?

Sapelo Island

Because of the kindness of a stranger, I was able to experience life on a remote unknown island off the coast of Georgia. I wasn't even aware that the island existed until a man named Henry invited us to come and stay. He said it was a place for healing.

Not anyone can travel to Sapelo Island; you either have to live there or be an invited guest. Tourists are not allowed. Sapelo Island, sparsely inhabited and not easily accessible, is both beautiful and historical.

Henry's house was beautiful, rustic and looked like a scene straight from a movie set. The structure stood on wooden stilts and had a large balcony, a porch swing, and a hammock. Huge oak trees covered in Spanish moss hung over the house, giving it an old southern feel.

Sapelo Island, a gift from a stranger, not only provided us with a new travel experience, but the greatest gift he gave us was the reminder of the goodness of others.

What's the best gift you have ever received or given?

Sapelo Island

Airport Herbs

Passing through Chicago's O'Hare International Airport, a busy hub full of florescent lighting and stressed-out people, I found a green sustainable garden growing among all the chaos and environmental pollutants.

The Rotunda Tower Garden won the Design and Construction Award for its indoor aeroponic garden that grows edible plants and herbs. The plants are then used in the restaurants within the airport. The material used to build the tower came from local recyclable structural steel, glass partitions, security doors, electrical panels, and furniture no longer needed by the airport.

This live, green environmentally friendly garden was a fresh and tasty stopover, providing a healthy sense of relief that even in urban USA, a plot of sustainable garden can still be found.

How can you be more environmentally friendly?

In what ways can you make a difference?

Fall Foods

In the Midwest, fall usually means a change in weather, dark cloudy days, and an end to warm sunshine. One way of making the most out of the changing seasons is to check out your local farmer's market.

On Saturday mornings while most people are sleeping, I grabbed some coffee and headed for the local market where I picked up some colorful autumn squashes and veggies.

I was reminded that all seasons change and that each season offers something new to enjoy.

How do the changing seasons affect you?

Can you appreciate what each season brings and celebrate its abundance?

Farmer's Market

Tea Meditation

You must be completely awake in the present to enjoy the tea.

Only in the awareness of the present, can your hands feel the pleasant warmth of the cup.

Only in the present, can you savor the aroma, taste the sweetness, appreciate the delicacy.

If you are ruminating about the past, or worrying about the future, you will completely miss the experience of enjoying the cup of tea.

You will look down at the cup, and the tea will be gone.
Life is like that.

If you are not fully present, you will look around and it will be gone.

You will have missed the feel, the aroma, the delicacy and beauty of life.

It will seem to be speeding past you. The past is finished.
Learn from it and let it go.

The future is not even here yet. Plan for it, but do not waste your time worrying about it.

Worrying is worthless.

When you stop ruminating about what has already happened, when you stop worrying about what might never happen, then you will be in the present moment.

Then you will begin to experience joy in life.

Thich Nhat Hanh.

Mindful Cup

The Art of Play

You don't have to go anywhere special to play. Play should be full of imagination and fun! If you are bored easily, then it's time to become more playful. Kids and cats know how to play in simple cardboard boxes.

When was the last time you acted really silly?

How can you incorporate more play into your life?

Mindful Moments

Practicing mindful moments creates a sense of peace and calm throughout your day.

Being mindful of your breath, posture, words, and surroundings will impact your life in ways to reward you mentally, emotionally and spiritually.

Today, make it a point to practice mindful moments.

How will you choose to be more mindful in one area of your life?

Start today to take five minutes to focus on your breath.

Find Inner Peace

Elvis Cake

In Memphis, Tennessee, I explored a variety of vegan restaurants. I ended up eating in a quirky, fun cafe that was 100% vegan. I had a delicious plant-based burger and a piece of Elvis cake for dessert which was made out of bananas, peanut butter, and chocolate. Elvis would have been proud!

What's the strangest thing you have ever baked or cooked?

Memphis

Big River Crossing

Big River Crossing, the country's longest active rail, bicycle, and pedestrian bridge extends a mile over the Mississippi river in Memphis, Tennessee and ends across the state line in Arkansas.

I rented a bike at the base of the bridge, which gave me the opportunity to see the Memphis skyline and watch a barge moving containers through the Mississippi Delta. I also met some fellow bikers crossing the river, one who said in passing that he had eaten a big meal of Mexican food before he started and said the beans helped him get over the river!

One of my dreams is to bike the rice paddies of Vietnam.

Do you have a dream to walk, ride, hike or ski?

How close are you to making your dream come true?

Mississippi River

Love Notes

There are so many ways to tell someone that you love them. One day I told my husband I loved him by leaving him a note on the spaghetti squash. Food is the language of love. Our homes need to be filled with love too.

How do you let loved ones know that you love them?

What are some simple ways you can let them know you care?

Forest Magic

Walking in the forest, I unexpectedly discovered this colorful creation that filled the dark autumn sky with color. The forest is known to hold magical energy and is a place of healing but finding this colorful art exhibit brought a bit of unexpected excitement into my life.

Inspiration can be found in the most unexpected places.

Where in life do you find inspiration?

How can you create magic for others to discover?

Magical Forest

How to Have a Happy Life!

Happiness comes in different ways. We all seek happiness but finding happiness in the small or everyday experiences is what life is all about.

Focus on things that bring you happiness in ways that you take for granted, such as a beloved pet, the sunshine, food on your table, a smile or simple silence. Practice being ok in the moment.

What can you do to not take happiness for granted?

What makes you the happiest?

How you share your happiness with others?

Search for Happiness Every Day

Pooped Out?

Winter can be a difficult time. The long dark days, cold nights, frigid air, and lack of sunshine can be draining.

Here are some helpful tips to get yourself through the seasonal change:

- Get a happy light
- Take vitamin D
- Wear colorful clothes
- Buy flowers
- Go to a salt spa
- Take a cat nap
- Paint a room yellow
- Cuddle with your cat or dog
- Eat colorful root vegetables

What restores your body and soul?

Take a Catnap

Searching Sedona

Surrounded by red rocks, whirling vortexes and positive energy, Sedona is a rare and beautiful spot on this earth.

Cathedral Rock is one of the larger vortex sites in Sedona. Vortexes are concentrations of energy spiraling upward from the Earth. As you climb the rock, you will see tree trunks that are twisted, a visual sign that energy is present. Vortex sites are known to have physical and spiritual healing properties and there are a number of them present in Sedona. Climbing to the top of Cathedral Rock was a challenge, but once there, was worth every step.

Is there a spiritual place that you seek to climb or discover?

How does this place nurture your soul?

Cathedral Rock

Death Valley Meditation

Death Valley is one of the most beautiful and diverse places I have ever traveled to. Expecting only barren desert, I was surprised to discover Ubehebe Crater, a large volcanic crater that measures nearly 600 feet deep and a half mile across. Although I was hiking with a group of people, I spent a few minutes meditating on the beauty and solitude of this beautiful place.

Meditation can take place anywhere and at any moment. Find a spot that feels peaceful and practice meditation for a few minutes a day. The peace that it brings you will affect every area of your life.

What brings you peace? How can you bring more of this into your daily life?

Take 5 minutes out of your day to begin a new meditation practice.

Begin a walking meditation alone, or with someone you care for.

Ubehebe Crater

Cloud Forest

A few years ago, I zip lined Monteverde Cloud Forest, the longest zip line over the rainforest canopy in Costa Rica. We took cable cars up the steep volcanic terrain, ascending into the cloudy forest. My adrenaline raced as I jumped off the platform and flew through the sky at tremendous speed. Excited, terrified, and in pain, I began the long journey back down to the ground as rain pelted my face like shards of glass. I could barely open my eyes as I sped from one zip lining station to the next.

Monteverde Cloud Forest zip line consists of 15 cables and 18 platforms. Views of the lake and Arenal Volcano are visible as you fly above the rainforest canopy. Although it wasn't my first-time zip lining, it was certainly one of the most adventurous life experiences that I have had.

What has been the most challenging or dangerous physical adventure that you have ever had?

How did it affect you and would you do it again?

When Your Cat Goes to Starbucks Without You

Some days, life just feels crazy and you need a good laugh. Today my cat took off in my car and didn't even bother to bring me back a drink. Bad boy!

What is something so absurd that it makes you laugh?

What can you do today to make someone else laugh?

Starbucks

Every day I Love You

Telling people that we love them isn't always easy when we get angry or upset with them, but sometimes in life we are not always given a second chance to forgive and have to live with unspoken words.

When is the last time that you told someone that you love them?

If it has been awhile since you said "I love you", what is stopping you?

PS: I love you!

> Every Day I Love You

I Love You More

Isolation

How is isolating good for us? For those of us who like to be social, isolation may be a welcome change in the beginning, but after a few days it may become difficult.

Personally, it's the initial adjustment of being alone and being restricted from some of my favorite places, but I know the pandemic won't last forever. I also know that using this time to make long needed personal changes is what I need to do at this time.

Use this time to do what you have put off or to do what you have wanted to do for years. Clean the house, take a hike, play with your pet, read a book, play drums, cook a favorite meal or dance.

Being alone and reflecting within is a healthy and necessary part of personal growth. Value this time to be fully present.

Do you spend enough time alone, or too much time alone?

Dance Through the Storm

Never has there been a time when the entire world has experienced such global isolation and lack of connection as during the 2020 pandemic.

For me, as my world becomes smaller and smaller, I have been forced within, something I am often too busy to do, or simply avoid. Now I find going within an essential part of my daily routine as my previous life no longer exists. I also know that like everything in life, this too shall pass and we will live in a new normal.

The storm clouds will pass, and the sun will shine again. Until then, **dance through the storm.**

How do you get through difficult times?

Can you find new ways to cope?

Look for the Rainbow

Corona Beauty

On one of my many daily walks, I came across white and blue flowers near the corner of the road. The flowers were tiny, yet beautiful and delicate. I snapped a photo and thought in the midst of all the life changing events, life continues to flourish. These tiny flowers were there as a reminder that our lives will continue to grow and be beautiful, although we may not always see it.

Although we may be separated from loved ones and our lives may feel as if they are falling apart or being uprooted, beauty is still there and surrounds us.

During difficult times, where can you find the beauty that is also present?

Purposely seek out all the beauty that exists all around you.

Flower Power

Costa Rican Kitchen

During a trip to Costa Rica, I was invited into one of the local's homes for a traditional Costa Rican meal. I was surprised at how simple yet efficient the kitchen was and loved the wood burning stove. The entire house had no windows but was totally open and exposed to outside elements.

I was served a wonderful Costa Rican meal of rice and beans by gracious hosts who spoke limited English. The experience was unlike any other that I have had on my travels, and it later inspired me to expand my cooking skills and be creative in the kitchen by cooking foods from around the world.

What is your favorite ethnic food?

When have you cooked it yourself or shared it with others?

Mother Earth Medicine

Mother earth heals body, mind, and spirit. There are no medicines more powerful than nature and there are so many natural ways of healing.

Walking barefoot on the ground is not only good for us, but it is healthy and grounding. Breathing in salt water into our lungs and feeling the sunshine on us are also healthy practices. Nature is powerful healing.

We are a part of the earth and return to it after our lives are completed. Being alive and connecting to nature is an important part of staying healthy.

How do you connect to nature?

How can you to make this kind of connection a part of your everyday life?

Connect to Mother Earth

Wild Tasty Asparagus

Last year was my first experience asparagus hunting. I remember slowly driving down country roads spotting wild asparagus growing in tall grasses, alongside fences and under trees. Food foraging soon became a treasure hunt for me as I took my prized asparagus home and cooked up a tasty feast.

What role does food play in your life?

How can you bring more natural foods into your everyday diet?

Wild Asparagus

Marvelous Morels

I first started going wild food hunting a few years ago and have to admit that I have become addicted. It's like a treasure hunt, as you never know what you will find.

With mushrooms, you really have to know your stuff as many mushrooms can be poisonous, but on a sunny Saturday morning, I found two large morel mushrooms hiding at the base of a large oak tree. I carefully cut the base of the mushrooms and headed home where we sautéed the mushrooms in garlic oil and added them to our favorite pasta.

Food foraging or hunting for wild foods isn't everyone's forte, but I love the adventure and can certainly appreciate the foods that I personally find and eat.

Where in your area can you go in search of wild foods?

Marvelous Mushrooms

Sweet Depression

In my private practice as a counselor, I have heard personal stories of sugar causing depression and low energy. Research indicates that sugar is not so sweet after all as it is linked to depression and other health issues.

The next time you reach for a candy bar or piece of cake, pay attention to how you feel physically, emotionally, and mentally both before and after you it. If your body is intolerant to sugar you will notice low energy, depression, and brain fog among other symptoms. If you are struggling with any of these symptoms take steps to reduce or eliminate sugar from your daily intake. This may be difficult at first, but your body and mind will thank you.

Life is meant to be sweet, but not too sweet.

Do you have an addiction to sugar?

How does it affect your mind and body?

Adventure Rocks

In communities around the country, people are painting and hiding rocks in attempts to make for a fun scavenger hunt. Rocks are painted with inspirational messages, humor, and beautiful designs. You never know what you are going to find. Half the fun is finding rocks and then re-hiding them so others can play too.

If you're not into group activities, you can still share your time or artwork for others to enjoy.

What kind of community groups, programs or activities are you involved in?

If you are not yet involved, where might you start?

Hopping Cool Frog

My Zendo

I had the opportunity to do something that I had always wanted to do, I practiced zazen, the art of walking and sitting meditation in Naples Zendo (Japanese meditation hall).

It may sound simple enough, but the practice of zazen is powerful in that when we enter into a state of Zen, we let go of all thoughts and mental clutter. In today's society, we can become stuck in our heads thinking about today, tomorrow, or the past. Zazen allows our minds to be still. We enter into a peaceful place of just being.

When did you last experience a state of mental peace and clarity?

How can you bring this practice into your life?

Zendo

Art and Soul

I started painting again after years of neglect, and once rediscovered my long-lost love.

In the past, I painted on huge canvases that I would build and stretch myself, but this time, I decided to work on a tiny scale and made a series of small paintings that measured 4×4 inches. I thought about what to paint and made the decision to paint a series of tiny birds.

Is there an old passion or hobby calling out to you to be explored?

What have you always wanted to try doing?

What, if anything, is holding you back?

Creative Flight

Fall Chaos

I've noticed over the years that fall seems to be a time of significant change for many. There appears to be loss, health issues, and abrupt endings.

As the leaves begin to fall and the earth prepares to go dormant for the long winter months, this is a time to let go of what is no longer needed. Sometimes we make those changes ourselves and other times it is forced upon us as we say goodbye to people we love, health issues arise, or things are out of our control.

In the northern hemisphere we see less light in the sky, the plants fade and return to the earth, and our bodies, minds, and spirit adjust to winter's dormancy. Wherever you are in life, embrace it, allow what needs to fall away or leave it go, and find joy and beauty in what is left.

What needs to fall away or leave your life?

Is Your Pet an Old Crank?

We all love cats and dogs as they provide years of companionship and enjoyment. I have a rescue cat named Lucky that I have had for over 11 years.

With aging pets, there come challenges, just as with people, as their health or habits change, or they become cranky with age. Regardless, my Lucky gets lots of love and attention as I take care of him in his old age.

Sometimes I get sad when I see how much he has aged and know that when the time comes that he leaves me, I will deeply mourn my beloved boy. Until then, I take the best care of him possible and am truly grateful for each day that we have together. Our unconditional love for each other will remain long after we say our goodbyes.

Do you have a pet?

How do you spend time with your pet?

Cranky Cat

How Do You See the World?

Do you see the world with rose colored glasses or do you see the world as an ugly place?

How we see the world around us often reflects the life that we live. Not that everything is perfect but finding the beauty in a sometimes-ugly world makes the difference between happiness and hope, or death and despair.

Whatever is happening in the world, we are free to choose how we view it. Remember that even in the ugliest of situations, there is always something beautiful being born.

Do you see beauty, or do you see ugliness in the world?

Can you change your perspective on how you see life?

Look at the World with a New Perspective

A Sign of Hope

A few years ago, I was living in the tropics and had traveled away for a short trip. I was making the 30-mile drive home from the airport when I saw a beautiful rainbow out of the window of my car and quickly snapped a picture.

It was a difficult time in my life, probably one of the hardest that I experienced alone, yet when I saw the rainbow, it gave me hope. I later read that rainbows are frequently represented as a sign of hope and promise of better times to come.

Believe in the power of hope, for tomorrow will be better and brighter than you can ever imagine.

What gives you hope?

When have you needed hope the most in your life?

How do you give others hope for the future?

Fort Myers, Florida

The End

Copyright © 2020 Tomorrow River Publishing

All rights reserved. This book or any portion thereof may not be reproduced or used in any manner whatsoever without the express written permission of the publisher except for the use of brief quotations in a book review.

Printed in the United States of America.

First Edition
First printing, December 2020

Book Design: Karolee Krause
Editing: Tim Krause

Tomorrow River Publishing
1017 Lindbergh Avenue
Stevens Point, WI 54481

www.tomorrowriverpublishing.com

ISBN: 9798580965338